P9-DIW-930

THE HERO SCHLIEMANN

THE DREAMER WHO DUG FOR TROY

LAURA AMY SCHLITZ
ILLUSTRATED BY ROBERT BYRD

CANDLEWICK PRESS
CAMBRIDGE, MASSACHUSETTS

The writing of this book was made possible, in part, by the
F. Parvin Sharpless Faculty and Curricular Advancement
Program at The Park School in Baltimore, Maryland.

Library of Congress Cataloging-in-Publication Data
Schlitz, Laura Amy
The hero Schliemann : The dreamer who dug for Troy /
Laura Amy Schlitz ; illustrated by Robert Byrd.
p. cm.
Includes bibliographical references.
ISBN-13: 978-0-7636-2283-1
ISBN-10: 0-7636-2283-4
1. Schliemann, Heinrich, 1822–1890—Juvenile literature.
2. Archaeologists—Germany—Biography—Juvenile literature. 3. Excavations
(Archaeology)—Greece—History—19th century—Juvenile literature.
4. Excavations (Archaeology)—Turkey—Troy (Extinct city)—Juvenile
literature. 5. Mycenae (Extinct city)—Juvenile literature. 6. Troy (Extinct
city)—Juvenile literature. 7. Greece—Civilization—To 146 B.C.—
Juvenile literature. I. Byrd, Robert, ill. II. Title.
DF212.S4S35 2006
930.1'092—dc22
[B] 2005046916

2 4 6 8 10 9 7 5 3 1

Printed in the United States of America

This book was typeset in Hightower and Trade Gothic.
The illustrations were done in ink and watercolor.

Candlewick Press
2067 Massachusetts Avenue
Cambridge, Massachusetts 02140

visit us at www.candlewick.com

For my parents, who nourished my dreams

L. A. S.

To Ginger

R. B.

·I·

Almost two hundred years ago, in Germany, a boy scratched his initials on a linden tree.

He was small for his age, with brown eyes and a head that looked too big for the rest of him. He was fifth in a family of nine children, and the oldest living son. Two and a half months after he was born, his older brother died and he was given the dead boy's name: Heinrich. The first initial, *H,* was two slashes and a crosspiece. He gripped the penknife tightly, trying to make the lines straight.

The next initial, *S,* was tricky. He knew that from experience: he had carved his initials dozens of times before, and the curves of the *S* were hard to control. Nevertheless, he wanted to make his mark. He started on the *S* of his last name.

• • •

His last name was Schliemann, and in the center of that German name is the English word *lie.* Perhaps now is as good a time as any to consider the subject of lying, because the boy Heinrich did not grow up to be a truthful man.

Few people are entirely honest. Many people lie once in a while. Heinrich Schliemann lied more often than that.

Heinrich Schliemann thought of his life as a story. He was the hero. He believed he was born under a lucky star, that he was meant to astonish the world with his adventures. From the time he was a boy—or so he said—he knew it was his destiny to dig up lost cities and find buried treasure.

And this is not impossible. It is children, after all, who dare to dream wild dreams. It is children who make up their minds that they will someday be rich and famous and that their lives will not be commonplace.

But most scholars believe that when sixty-year-old Heinrich Schliemann wrote his autobiography, he rewrote his life, giving himself the kind of childhood a hero ought to have had. Because Schliemann was an imaginative and convincing liar, it's hard to know what really happened and what he made up.

He was a man who loved stories. He loved them so much that he wanted them to be true.

• • •

Heinrich Schliemann was born in 1822. His father was a clergyman, the pastor of a little village named Ankershagen. It was his childhood home, Schliemann wrote, that awakened his love for "the mysterious and the marvelous." The little village of Ankershagen was riddled with stories. Close to the Schliemann parsonage, a wicked robber had buried his dead child in a golden cradle. "Behind our garden," Schliemann wrote, "was a pond . . . out of which a maiden was believed to rise each midnight, holding a silver bowl. . . . My faith in . . . these treasures was so great that, whenever I heard my father complain of his poverty, I always expressed my astonishment that he did not dig up the silver bowl or the golden cradle and so become rich."

Schliemann's story about these folk tales may be true—or it may not. The legends about the golden cradle and the silver bowl are authentic Ankershagen stories; Schliemann did not make them up, and he may have known of them when he was a boy. All his life he was fascinated by what lay buried: by bones and graveyards and treasure. It is also possible that Heinrich only read the stories later in his life. There were books of Ankershagen folk tales in his library when he was a man.

According to Schliemann, his love for the poet Homer also began in childhood. At the age of seven, he received a Christmas present from his father, a children's book based on Homer's epic poem *The Iliad*. Inside the book was a picture of the ancient city of Ilium, or Troy. Heinrich was much struck by the towering walls of the city. "Father," he insisted, "if such walls once existed, they cannot possibly have been completely destroyed."

Heinrich's father tried to explain to his son that the city of Troy had been burned to the ground and that no one alive knew where the city had been. But Heinrich would not listen. It was then that he decided that he would someday search the world for the lost city of Troy and dig it out of the ground.

Is the story of the Christmas gift—and what it inspired—true? Who can say? *The Iliad* is a story of courage, violence, and splendor—the kind of story that can set the imagination on fire. And a copy of the children's book *was* found in Heinrich's library when he was grown up, and Heinrich's name *was* written inside—but in the handwriting of an adult. Only one thing is certain: if seven-year-old Schliemann dreamed of finding lost Troy, his dreams were abruptly set aside. When Heinrich was nine years old, his whole world changed.

• • •

Ernst Schliemann, Heinrich's father, was a poor excuse for a man of God. He was quarrelsome and violent. He drank too much and spent large sums of money on presents for a woman who was not his wife. The people of Ankershagen suspected him of mishandling money that belonged to the church. They disapproved of him and felt sorry for his wife.

When Heinrich was nine years old, his mother died and the people of Ankershagen began to show Pastor Schliemann how they felt about him. They took to marching around the Schliemann house every Sunday, banging on pots and pans and throwing stones. The village children were no longer allowed to play with the young Schliemanns.

Heinrich felt a special grief in losing touch with a little girl who was his friend, Minna Meincke. Heinrich and Minna had vowed that one day they would marry and devote their lives to searching for treasure. In his autobiography, Heinrich wrote that no trouble in his adult life caused him as much pain as "my separation from my little bride."

Little bride? When Heinrich Schliemann was writing his autobiography, tales of childhood romance were considered very touching. The tale of Minna may have been one of Heinrich's prettiest stories. He did, however, ask Minna to marry him fifteen years later.

Heinrich's ninth year was a hard one. His mother was dead, his father was disgraced, and he was sent away to live with an uncle, who arranged for his education.

In the years that followed, Heinrich's father lost his job, and the family grew poorer. It was decided that Heinrich, as the eldest son, should leave school and earn his own living. At this time, he was fourteen years old, a slight and weedy-looking boy with a hollow chest. None of Heinrich's school reports give any hint that the schoolboy was a genius. His grades were only so-so.

He spent the next five years working for a grocer named Ernst Holtz. The work was both strenuous and dull. From five in the morning to eleven at night, Heinrich unpacked heavy barrels of goods. His muscles ached, and his mind was numb with boredom. Worst of all, he felt trapped: the future held nothing but more of the same.

It was ill health that saved him. One day he lifted a heavy cask of chicory and began to cough up blood. Coughing up blood is a symptom of tuberculosis, a deadly disease that was widespread in the 1800s. Heinrich feared that unless he found less taxing work, the disease would kill him.

And so Heinrich left the grocer's shop behind. A change of climate was often prescribed as a cure for tuberculosis, and Heinrich had an itch to travel, to escape to another land. He hastened to his father's house and begged for money to take a journey. Ernst Schliemann refused.

Heinrich made up his mind to leave Ankershagen and strike out for himself. He was not to see his childhood home for eleven years.

·II·

Heinrich's first journey took him to the German port of Hamburg. It was the beginning of a lifelong passion for traveling. Heinrich wrote: "The view of Hamburg . . . carried me off to seventh heaven. . . . I turned into a dreamer." His dream, at this point in his life, was to regain his health and to rise in the world.

Unfortunately, he couldn't find work. No one wanted an employee who coughed up blood. At last Heinrich grew so poor that he wrote to ask his uncle for help. His uncle sent money with a letter that shamed Heinrich so deeply that he promised himself: "I would never again ask a relative for aid; rather would I starve to death than beg such a man for the loan of a bread crumb."

He kept that promise. He also kept the money. Shortly afterward, he heard there was a ship sailing to

South America, and the prospect of a job in La Guaira, Venezuela. The ship's agent accepted Heinrich's application gratefully. It was not easy to find young men who were willing to travel two thousand miles to a land that was best known as a breeding ground for yellow fever.

On November 27, 1841, the ship *Dorothea* "flew like a seabird over the dark foamy waves." Heinrich was bound for South America.

But he never got there. The weather was stormy, with high winds and temperatures below zero. Around midnight on December 10, Heinrich was awakened by the captain's shouts. Waves dashed against the boat with such force that the portholes were shattered, and water gushed in. "I barely saved my life running almost naked on deck," wrote Schliemann. He lashed himself to the ship's railing so that he wouldn't be swept overboard. Snowflakes fell from the sky. He said a silent farewell to his family, prayed to God, and "gave my body over to the sharks." The ship began to sink.

Then, suddenly, Heinrich's fear was swept away. He untied himself and began to climb the rigging, determined to postpone death as long as possible. As he was climbing, the broken ship rocked and pitched, sinking deep below the waves. Heinrich grabbed hold of a floating barrel. He lost consciousness. Some hours later, he awoke and found himself on a sandbank off the Dutch coast. His body was covered with bruises and deep gashes, and two of his teeth had been knocked out—but he was alive.

Fearsome though the shipwreck was, it left Heinrich feeling optimistic. Only three men survived the wreck of the *Dorothea.* "God must have chosen me for great things," he wrote. "I felt reborn." And it is a curious fact that after his shipwreck, Heinrich was seldom troubled by ill health. He took up sea bathing. He stopped coughing up blood. Though he was a small man all his life, he was tough and hardy—and his energy was boundless.

When Heinrich Schliemann made his way from the coast to the city of Amsterdam, he was penniless. He spoke no Dutch, and he didn't know a soul in the city. Nevertheless, he decided to settle there.

He found work as a kind of grown-up errand boy, carrying messages and bills around town. He lived in an attic room—freezing cold in the winter, stiflingly hot in summer. Solitary study was his only amusement, as he could not afford to go to concerts or plays. "Friendships were made in coffee-houses," wrote Schliemann, "and since I did not visit any, I had no friend."

He spent every idle moment in study. He came to realize that he had a gift for languages. He memorized long passages from French and English novels, which he recited aloud. When he came to a hard passage, he shouted at the top of his lungs. Landlords and neighbors did not appreciate the Schliemann method for learning languages—several times he was forced to find new lodgings—but he persisted. He taught himself French, English, Dutch, Spanish, Italian, and Portuguese.

It must have been a lonely life, but Heinrich did not pity himself. He drew strength from his belief that he was destined for great things; he was a hero, fighting his way to fortune.

He found a better job. He became a bookkeeper for the firm of Messrs. B. H. Schröder and Company. Though Schröder and Company traded extensively with Russia, no one spoke the language. Within six weeks, Heinrich taught himself enough Russian to write letters for the firm. By 1846, he had become the Russian agent for Schröder and Company, and moved to St. Petersburg, where he was "crowned with the fullest success." Russian traders seemed to like the cocky young man who had mastered their language so quickly.

Heinrich was now twenty-four years old. Five years before, he had been a penniless nobody. Now he was a prosperous merchant, and ready to marry. He wrote to the Meincke family, only to learn that his darling Minna had already married. The older Schliemann wrote that this was "the greatest disaster" that could have befallen him.

Still, he was not altogether wretched. He loved his home in St. Petersburg. He traveled widely, going to London and Paris, Brussels, Hamburg, and Berlin. And he was earning more money all the time.

All his life, Heinrich Schliemann craved money. He never took it for granted. Even when he was a millionaire, he was stingy with small sums of money. He liked staying in grand hotels, but he always stayed on the top floor, where the rooms were cheapest: he would rather climb six flights of stairs than pay for a room lower down. He always carried his own trunk—why waste a dollar on a porter? He could not bear for anyone to cheat him.

On the other hand, he could be both generous and extravagant. He had a weakness for well-tailored clothes and spent a surprising amount of money to have his shirts regularly cleaned and starched. He was endlessly loyal to his family, sending ever-increasing amounts of money to his brothers, sisters, and father.

In 1850, Heinrich learned that his brother Ludwig had died of typhoid fever in California. Ludwig Schliemann was one of the many treasure seekers who headed to California during the Gold Rush. Heinrich went to America to settle his brother's debts and to make sure that Ludwig had a proper gravestone. Graves were always important to Heinrich—but he had another reason for going to California. Ludwig had made it clear that there were fortunes to be made in the Gold Rush. If there was money to be had, Heinrich wanted his share. Though he criticized the Californians for their "swindling," "cunning," and "immense love of money," he was their equal in every way.

One of Heinrich's oddest lies was contrived in California. In his diary, he wrote a vivid eyewitness account of the San Francisco fire, which he claimed took place in June 1851. The fire actually took place in May, when Heinrich was elsewhere. It seems that Heinrich read about the fire in the newspapers and decided to write about it as if he had been there. He wrote his version of the story on a single sheet of paper and glued it into his diary so cunningly that it looks like one of the diary pages.

This was a bizarre thing to do. He was not just showing off. Heinrich lied in his *diary*. Once again, he was changing the details of his life in order to fabricate a better story. As the hero of the story, he felt that he belonged at the Great Fire.

Heinrich's time in California was not wasted. He opened a bank and traded in gold dust. During the Gold Rush years, California was a hotbed of crime and disease. Heinrich, who was finicky about cleanliness, hated it—but he stayed in California long enough to double his fortune.

His journey home was catastrophic. When Heinrich reached the Atlantic coast of Panama, he learned that his ship had just left for Europe. There would be no other ship for weeks to come. He was stranded in a place where there was no shelter and no food.

It rained without stopping for two weeks. The land teemed with scorpions and rattlesnakes. Heinrich camped under the palm trees with 2,500 other wretched travelers. No one had dry clothes, and there was no way to kindle a fire. A few resourceful souls were able to kill monkeys, iguanas, and turtles, which had to be eaten raw. Hundreds of people died. The mosquitoes gnawed at the survivors, making sleep impossible. Heinrich wrote, "I lay more dead than alive. . . . In this horrible situation all human feeling forsook us. . . . Crimes were perpetuated among us; *crimes so terrible!* that . . . I cannot think of it without cold and trembling horror."

He never explained what the crimes were. But once again, Heinrich survived. He was alive and kicking when the next ship came. He paid for a cabin onboard without haggling over the price, gulped down beef tea, and slept in dry bedclothes for the first time in two weeks. Once again, luck had sustained him, and he sailed home to St. Petersburg with a fortune and no injury worse than a wounded leg.

·III·

When Heinrich returned to Russia, he began to think seriously about marriage. He proposed to several women, all of whom rejected him. At last his choice fell on Ekaterina Petrovna Lyshina, the daughter of a business acquaintance. Heinrich had proposed to Ekaterina before his trip to America, but she had refused him. Heinrich was not attractive to women, with his small frame and round head. During his journey, he had grown no better-looking; he had, however, become very rich. Ekaterina accepted the millionaire's proposal, and they were married.

It was a bitterly unhappy marriage. Heinrich married for love. Ekaterina married for money. Neither of them got what they wanted. Heinrich nagged and scolded his wife over every penny she spent. Ekaterina grew to hate the sight of her husband. In spite of their misery, they had three children: a son named Sergei, born in 1855, and two daughters, Natalia and Nadezhda, born in 1858 and 1861.

During the next eleven years, Heinrich made more and more money. He continued to invest in groceries and luxuries. He bought large supplies of saltpeter, brimstone, and lead to sell to the Russian military during the Crimean War. "All through the war," Heinrich admitted, "I thought of nothing but money." His greatest solace was study. When he was not increasing his fortune, he continued to teach himself languages: Slovenian, Danish, Swedish, Norwegian, Polish, Latin, and Greek.

It was Greek that led him to a new world. From the very first, his relationship with the Greek language was a love affair. He was drunk with the beauty of the words. "How is it possible for any language to be so noble!" he wondered. He filled thirty-five copybooks with exercises in Greek. He read and reread Homer's poems *The Iliad* and *The Odyssey* until he knew long sections by heart. Homer's world of heroic splendor captured his imagination so totally that he carried the books with him wherever he went.

Heinrich began to tire of business. In his exercise books, he wrote, "I cannot remain a merchant any longer." And: "How is it that I who have made three fortunes am so miserably unhappy?"

The decision to give up business was not an easy one. His success in the marketplace assured him that he was worthwhile—a man of substance. Outside the world of business, he was a nobody once more. He would have to invent himself all over again.

He began his new life by circling the globe. He visited countries that were all but unknown to most Europeans. During his world tour, he put up with bad weather, rough roads, and nasty food, but high prices never failed to rouse his sense of outrage.

On the sea voyage from Japan to California, he wrote his first book, *China and Japan in Present Times.* Once back in Europe, he passed through London and visited the Crystal Palace Park at Sydenham. There he saw copies of Egyptian temples, stone tools from a cave in France, and life-size models of dinosaurs. The next day he prowled the halls of the British Museum, looking at antiquities from Egypt and Mesopotamia.

His growing curiosity about the ancient world was not unusual for a man of his time. Heinrich was living in an age when the general public was becoming more knowledgeable about the distant

past. “Prehistory”—the study of human beings before the invention of writing—was a new science. All over fashionable Europe, the ancient world had become the latest craze.

Heinrich was attracted by this new science, though he had not yet decided to become an archaeologist. He felt torn between the worlds of business and scholarship. He enrolled in the French university, the Sorbonne, but took time away from his classes to mount guard over his fortune. When he heard about economic opportunities in the United States, he headed for America. The year was 1867, and the slaves had been freed for four years.

Once in the United States, Heinrich found him-

Timeline: A New Idea of History

1710 and 1748
Early excavations at Herculaneum and Pompeii. For centuries these ancient cities were hidden beneath volcanic ash. When archaeologists uncover them, the public is enchanted by the beauty of the “Pompeii style.”

1822
Jean-François Champollion pu lishes his “Letter to Monsieur Dacier,” explaining his new ins into Egyptian hieroglyphs. For centuries, people had marvele over Egyptian monuments—b no one had ever been able to read the writing on the walls. Champollion had broken the c

1800
Lord Elgin wrests the marble statues from the Parthenon, a temple sacred to the Greek goddess Athena. The statues are displayed in London and cause an artistic sensation.

self deeply moved by the ambition and intelligence of the former slaves. He wrote that any statements about the laziness of Negro freedmen were "downright falsehoods. . . . They are as willing and eager to work . . . as any workmen I have yet seen and . . . both morally and intellectually, they stand much higher than their former tyrants." He sympathized with the former slaves' struggle to create a new and a better life. He had never forgotten what it was to be an underdog.

Heinrich celebrated his forty-sixth birthday alone, in New York City. Though he did not yet realize it, he was about to set off on a heroic quest: a lifelong search for the lost city of Troy.

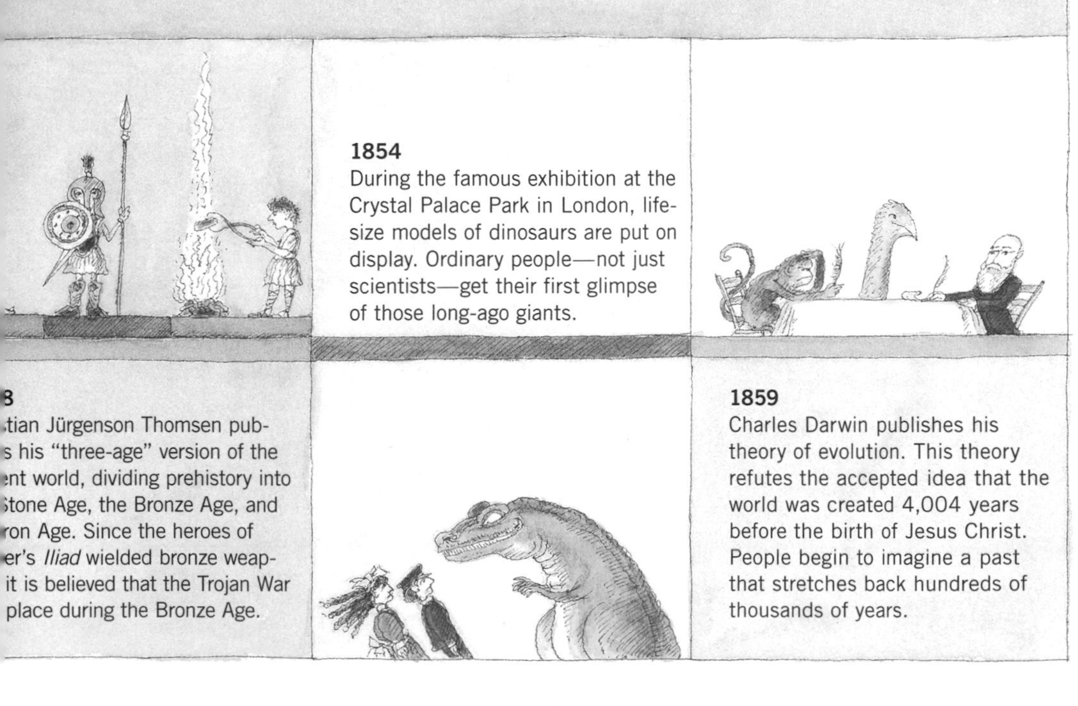

HEINRICH SCHLIEMANN'

1. Aachen
2. Tunis
3. Alexandria
4. Bologna
5. Florence
6. Naples
7. Pompeii
8. Capri
9. Paestum
10. Marseilles
11. Paris
12. Würzburg
13. Alexandria
14. Cairo
15. Ceylon
16. Madras
17. Calcutta
18. Delhi
19. Mushoori
20. Agra
21. Lucknow
22. Mirzapoor
23. Singapore
24. Jakarta
25. Java
26. Saigon
27. Canton
28. Hong Kong
29. Shanghai
30. Tientsin
31. Peking
32. Yokohama
33. Tokyo
34. San Francisco
35. Nicaragua
36. Havana
37. Mexico City
38. London
39. Paris
North America
Atlantic
Ocea
Pacific Ocean
South America
N
W
E
S
34
35
36
37

World Tour 1864–1865
Russia
Asia
Europe
Japan
China
India
Africa
Indian Ocean
Australia

·IV·

Most modern scholars think that it was not until the age of forty-six that Heinrich Schliemann made up his mind to look for Troy, the lost city of Homer's *Iliad.* Before 1868, there is nothing about finding Troy in the thousands of letters and papers written by Heinrich Schliemann. If—as Heinrich maintained later in life—he had dreamed of finding the lost city since he was seven years old, it was a dream he had never shared. It was a dream he had buried as deep as Troy itself.

And it was a peculiar dream. Most of the scholars of Schliemann's day doubted whether Troy was a real place. Homer's war poem *The Iliad* was considered the greatest epic of all time, but it was considered to be fictional, an invented tale. Troy was a place in a *story,* like Oz or Narnia or Neverland.

Heinrich, of course, wanted the story to be true. He wanted to believe that the Trojan War was a real war that happened just the way Homer said it did. If current scholarship held that Troy was a myth, the scholars were wrong. Heinrich preferred the historians of ancient Greece.

The ancient Greek writers believed that there had once been a great war between the Greeks and the Trojans. Greek historians like Thucydides (c. 460–400 BCE) and Herodotus (c. 484–425 BCE) considered the Trojan War part of their ancient history, and although they couldn't be sure exactly when it occurred, they agreed that it took place roughly eight hundred years before their time, around 1250 BCE. Greek historians came up with these dates by keeping track of family histories and stories: "Let's see, my grandfather said his grandfather said *his* grandfather said . . ." This is not the most accurate way to keep track of historic events, but the Trojan War took place before the Greeks adopted an alphabet from the Phoenicians and began to write.

The ancient Greek historians also agreed that Homer lived four to six hundred years after the Trojan War. It is most likely that Homer's two great works, *The Iliad* and *The Odyssey,* were composed orally and sung by bards. During the seventh century, the Greeks became fully literate, and different versions of the poems were tacked together and written down.

Who Was Homer?

Homer was the greatest poet of the ancient world. According to tradition, he lived nearly three thousand years ago. He was said to have been blind: in ancient Greece, blind men often became storytellers. When we speak of those two astonishing poems, The Iliad *and* The Odyssey, *we say they are "by Homer."*

Homer is a mysterious figure. Everyone agrees on his genius—but no one is sure whether or not he ever lived. Some scholars think that the poems were composed by many men, over hundreds of years. Heinrich Schliemann believed in a single "Homer"—the blind poet of legend.

According to many scholars, Homer never wrote a line of poetry. During his lifetime, the Greeks had no alphabet. The great poems were created, learned by heart, and chanted aloud. This must have been a staggering feat of memorization—both The Iliad *and* The Odyssey *are so long, it would take several days to recite them.*

Homer's two masterpieces are very different. The Iliad *is the tale of the warriors who fought in the Trojan War, particularly the doomed and defiant Achilles and his enemy, the noble Hector.* The Odyssey, *which takes place after the invasion of Troy, is an adventure story. It follows Odysseus, the craftiest of the Greek warriors, on his journey home to Ithaca.*

By the time Heinrich Schliemann was born, European historians had come to question the entire existence of a poet named Homer. They even wondered whether there had been a Trojan War. Above all, they wondered how much truth could be left in a story after it had been told and retold for hundreds of years. Scholars reasoned that if there had ever been any historic truth to *The Iliad,* it had long ago been lost.

Heinrich, of course, did not reason that way. In matters that touched on Homer, Heinrich did not reason: he was ruled by his imagination and his heart. He

worshiped Homer and adored *The Iliad*, and he believed that if Homer's poem sang of a city of Troy near the Dardanelles, it was a real city. If Heinrich followed the clues in Homer's poems very carefully, he might be able to find the ruins of that city and bring it to light.

Heinrich's visit to "the fatherland of my darling Homer" began in 1868, with a visit to Corfu, the Greek island where the shipwrecked Odysseus met the princess Nausikaa. In *The Odyssey,* Odysseus meets the princess by the River Cressida, where she is washing clothes

with her maids. Because Odysseus is naked, he holds a branch in front of his loins. Heinrich followed the same path, and suffered the same embarrassment as Homer's hero. In order to cross the river, he took off his trousers. A number of women in a nearby field stopped work long enough to have a good giggle at the German businessman in his underwear. It seems likely that Heinrich was, in a private, middle-aged way, *playing* Odysseus—and it was a good role for him. Odysseus was a crafty man, quick to invent a tale, a traveler who had been shipwrecked and stranded.

After Corfu, Heinrich followed Odysseus back to his homeland—Ithaca. Unlike Troy, Ithaca was a name that could be found on any map. *Whether* Odysseus ever lived was a matter of opinion, but there was no question as to *where* he lived: Odysseus was king of Ithaca. There were even guidebooks that gave locations for "Odysseus's palace" and other Homeric sites. Heinrich was exactly the kind of tourist for whom these books were written. He walked in his hero's footsteps and shed tears at the sites where Odysseus once wept.

He also did his first digging. He dug in the ground where folk memory placed the palace of Odysseus. Here he found five or six vases filled with ashes. Since the Greeks in Homer's poem cremated their dead and buried the ashes in vases, Heinrich's fancy took a giant leap. "It is very possible that I have in my five little vases the bodies of Odysseus and Penelope." It was his first excavation, and one that was to prove characteristic. He followed the story, delved into the earth, and leaped to ecstatic conclusions about whatever he found.

After this heady discovery, Heinrich proceeded to Mycenae, the stronghold of Agamemnon. It was said that the warrior-king of *The Iliad* lay buried there, though his tomb had never been found. Heinrich admired the famous lion-carved gates of the Mycenean kings and braved the bats in Agamemnon's treasury. He spent the next week exploring the Greek islands, before proceeding to Bunarbashi, a Turkish village near the Dardanelles.

Heinrich was not the only man in Europe who believed in a real Trojan War and a real Troy. Though he was in the minority, he was not alone. Other scholars who had considered the matter had concluded that Homer's Troy might lie beneath the village of Bunarbashi. Heinrich decided to see for himself.

From the first, Heinrich was disappointed by Bunarbashi. For one thing, it was dirty, which offended his tidy soul. For another, it was ten miles from the sea. Heinrich, who knew much of *The Iliad* by heart, remembered that the Greek warriors went back and forth from their ships to the city several times a day. If the distance between the two points was ten miles, this would be impossible. He also recalled the famous scene in *The Iliad* in which the Greek hero Achilles chased the Trojan prince Hector around the walled city. Heinrich tried to act out the chase and failed. The hill was so steep that he could get around it only by crawling on all fours. Heinrich was perplexed: *Homer could not have been mistaken about the chase.* Since Homer could not be wrong, Troy must lie on some other hill. After a cursory dig, Heinrich abandoned Bunarbashi for the plain of Hissarlik.

Heinrich was by no means the first to consider Hissarlik as a possible site for Troy. For the last hundred years, there had been scholars who suspected that Troy was at Hissarlik rather than Bunarbashi. One of these men was an archaeologist named Frank Calvert. It was Frank Calvert who first discovered that what looked like a large hill on the Turkish plain was actually a mound made by human beings. Frank Calvert believed that inside that mound lay the lost city of Troy. He bought some of the land and started digging.

BCE?
Letters + Numbers = Dates

Throughout this book, dates are given in terms of the Common Era. The "Common Era" is a new way of talking about historic dates. American and European historians have traditionally used a calendar based on Christianity. Events of ancient history—like the Trojan War—were given a "BC" after the number, meaning, "before Christ." Things that happened after the birth of Christ were labeled "AD" for "anno Domine"*—Latin words for "in the year of Our Lord."*

Common Era dating uses the same numbers, but different initials after the dates. What used to be called 5 BC (five years before Christ) is now called 5 BCE (five years before the Common Era.) Historians use Common Era dates as a way of being courteous to people of all religions. Common Era dates are also more accurate, since it is not certain exactly when Jesus Christ lived.

When Heinrich met Frank Calvert in 1868, he adopted Calvert's beliefs: "I completely shared Frank Calvert's conviction that the plateau of Hissarlik marks the site of ancient Troy."

Heinrich gave Hissarlik the same "tests" he had administered at Bunarbashi. He concluded that Hector and Achilles could easily have run the nine miles around this mound. He was delighted to discover a ruined temple, a nearby swamp, and a mountain range in the distance—all of which reminded him of landscapes in *The Illiad.* "The beautiful hill of Hissarlik grips one with astonishment," he wrote later. "That hill seems to be destined by nature to carry a great city." All of the clues in *The Iliad* seemed now to point to Hissarlik as the site of ancient Troy. Heinrich was so excited that he ordered a chicken dinner to celebrate. Unfortunately, the chicken who was to be the main course objected to the whole idea and ran for its life, squawking in panic. Heinrich, who had a soft spot for animals, paid the owner to set the chicken free and sat down to a poultry-free supper in high good humor.

Heinrich Schliemann is famous for "finding Troy." Many people give him credit for being the first to look for Troy in the right place—but by right, that honor belongs to Frank Calvert. If Heinrich Schliemann had not met Frank Calvert on his journey, he might never have excavated at Hissarlik. The admission "I . . . shared Frank Calvert's opinion" changed gradually to "Frank Calvert, the famous archaeologist . . . shares *my* opinion. . . ." Eventually Heinrich, who admitted that he was "a braggart and a bluffer," made the discovery sound as if it were his alone.

Frank Calvert, however, was a remarkably generous man. He must have realized that Heinrich had the energy, as well as the money, to organize a large-scale excavation. He gave Heinrich the benefit of his archaeological knowledge and explained how to get permission to dig from the Turkish government. Heinrich promised to return to Hissarlik the following year, permission in hand.

·V·

The years 1868 and 1869 were remarkable ones in Heinrich's life. He retired from business, appointed himself Homer's champion, and divorced his wife.

He began to dream of a Greek bride: dark-haired, interested in Homer, and—if possible—beautiful. He had no desire for a rich bride. He knew he was not handsome, and he hoped to make up for it with a well-padded wallet and a knowledge of foreign languages. He told his Greek tutor, Theokletos Vimpos, that he wanted his future wife to love learning "because otherwise she cannot love and respect me." Above all, he wished for "a good and loving heart."

As it happened, Theokletos had an unmarried niece: dark-haired, bookish, and poor. Sophia Engastromenos was only sixteen years old when her photograph was sent to the forty-seven-year-old millionaire. Her youth frightened Heinrich. He was afraid that so young a girl would have her heart set on romance. But Sophia's photograph enchanted him, and at last he declared that he had fallen in love.

Having fallen in love with Sophia, it only remained to meet her. The Engastromenos family was excited by the prospect of having a millionaire in the family, and Sophia was bundled into her sister's best dress. When Heinrich spoke to her alone, he asked her point-blank, "Why do you wish to marry me?" Sophia replied, "Because my parents have told me that you are a rich man!"

Heinrich flew into a temper and marched back to his hotel room to sulk. The Engastromenos family huddled around Sophia, begging her to send a letter of apology. Sophia wrote that she had not meant to offend her suitor; she had answered honestly because she believed that he wanted the truth.

Heinrich forgave her. By this time, he was head over heels in love. For the second time in his life, he married a woman he had barely met, a woman whose family was in need of money. This time, his wife was thirty years younger than himself—Sophia was so young that she smuggled her dolls along on her honeymoon.

Poor Sophia! During the first months of married life, Heinrich dragged her to museums all over Europe. She preferred the circus. He lavished expensive gifts upon her, supervised her diet, and drew up a gymnastics program that he thought would keep her healthy. He pestered her to learn foreign languages. She suffered from headaches, stomachaches, and homesickness.

And yet the marriage was not a disaster. Sophia Schliemann was loving and wise beyond her years. She relieved Heinrich's deep loneliness. She made up her mind that "Henry" was a genius and that geniuses were not quite like other people. She even awakened a streak of playfulness in his nature—on their honeymoon in Venice, he dived headfirst out of a gondola in order to make her laugh. She called him her "friend for life" and "dearest husband."

As for "Henry," his love and respect for Sophia increased as he came to know her better. To him, she was his "adored wife and everlasting friend." He admired her mind as well as her beauty and concluded, "I knew I loved and needed a woman of her grandeur."

In 1871, Sophia gave birth to a baby girl who was christened Andromache, after the Trojan princess in *The Iliad*. Shortly after Andromache's birth, Heinrich received the *firman*, or permission, he had been seeking from the Turkish government. The terms of the agreement were simple: Heinrich was responsible for all expenses. If artifacts were found, half of them were to be given to the new museum in Constantinople. A supervisor was appointed to keep a watchful eye on the amateur archaeologist. Heinrich disliked the man and grumbled over having to pay his salary.

When Heinrich began digging at Hissarlik, he had very little idea what he was doing. He knew that he wanted to dig into the mound and find a city of the Bronze Age, but he didn't know what a Bronze Age city would look like. His guide was Homer—he was looking for artifacts and architecture that matched the descriptions in Homer's poetry. This was not a scientific approach.

The thrust of his plan was to dig—deep. At the top of the mound, he expected to find a Roman city, then a Greek city underneath, then a Greek city from the time of Homer, and, just below that, the walled city of *The Iliad*. Instead of carefully sifting through the mound, layer by layer, he decided to dig out vast trenches—rather as if he were removing slices from a cake. Since Homer's Troy was ancient, Heinrich expected to find it near the bottom.

And so he dug, violently and impatiently. Frank Calvert advised him to proceed with care, to sift through what he was throwing away, but Heinrich was not a cautious man. He whacked away at the mound as if it were a piñata.

Modern archaeologists do not dig like this. They remove the earth gently and keep detailed records of what they find. If they find an artifact that isn't what they're hoping to find, they don't discard the artifact: they change their ideas. Instead of looking *for* something, they examine whatever comes to light. Heinrich, of course, was looking for Homer's Troy. "Troy . . . was sacked twice," modern archaeologists remark, "once by the Greeks and once by Heinrich Schliemann." It is generally agreed that Schliemann did more damage than the Greeks.

His early finds were not very interesting. He discovered the remains of a wall. He found coins, a few bones, the clay whorls that women used in spinning thread. Later there were little objects made of clay, which he thought were "owl-headed" vases, sacred to Athena. He was looking for weapons like the "pitiless bronze" spears described by Homer—but the weapons he found were made of stone. Heinrich was bewildered. He was seeking the remains of a great city. Where was the bronze armor, the palaces and jewels?

Spring turned to summer. The climate of Hissarlik tends to extremes—bitter cold in winter, blistering heat in summer, and a wind that never stops blowing.

Since Homer sang of "windy Troy," Heinrich had once rejoiced that Hissarlik was windy, but his enthusiasm for high winds was waning. Gusts of air blew grit into his eyes. Dust scratched his skin and filled his mouth when he tried to speak.

As the workmen dug, they unearthed thousands of poisonous snakes. Hissarlik was also home to scorpions and mosquitoes. At night, it was difficult to sleep: there were so many shrieking owls and croaking frogs. Poisonous centipedes invaded the Schliemann bed.

The workmen grew weary of hauling heavy wheelbarrows full of earth. They began to work more slowly, frequently pausing to smoke. Heinrich badgered them about their smoking. He believed that smoking wasted time and weakened the body.

Heinrich had become an unpaid doctor. He hated dirt and disease, and could not see either without wanting to meddle. He gave the workers quinine in order to prevent malaria. He preached the virtues of exercise, fresh fruit, and sea bathing.

Heinrich was particularly proud of curing a girl of seventeen. She was almost too weak to walk, she coughed uncontrollably, and her body was covered with ulcers. Heinrich was shocked by her frailty and the filthy rags she wore. He called for castor oil and administered a dose; he also asked Sophia to give the girl a pretty dress from her own wardrobe. He taught his patient a few simple exercises and told her to take daily sea baths. A month later, she walked three miles to kiss the dusty shoes of "Dr. Schliemann." Her cough was gone, and the ulcers were healed. She was happy and strong.

Heinrich was touched by her gratitude, but—as he often complained—he had come to Hissarlik to excavate Troy, not to play doctor. He urged the workers to dig deeper, to go faster.

The first season ended. Heinrich hired more workmen. He was beginning to understand the way the mound was layered. Little by little, he came to distinguish between the ruins of four different cities—cities that lay on top and outside of another, like nesting dolls or the layers of an onion.

In an onion, however, the layers are orderly. At Hissarlik, the layers are uneven and the boundaries overlap. The site would have confounded a far more experienced archaeologist than Heinrich Schliemann. "It was an entirely new world for me," confessed Heinrich. "I had to learn everything by myself."

During the second season, Heinrich found a panel of carved marble that showed the sun god in his chariot. Though the panel, which dates from between 355 and 281 BCE, was not old enough to belong to Homer's Troy, it was the largest and most beautiful object yet found—and it was found on Frank Calvert's land.

Stratification
The Layers of History

When Heinrich Schliemann dug at Hissarlik, he was hoping to find Homer's city of Troy. Instead, he found many cities, one on top of the other. Sorting out the different layers, or strata, was a difficult job.

In order to understand Heinrich's work, imagine that you've tossed everything that you've ever owned into a heap in the middle of the floor. On top of the mound would be the clothes you wore yesterday. Lower down, the clothes would be smaller. Legos and puzzle pieces would get bigger. At the bottom of the mound would be baby clothes, board books, and rattles.

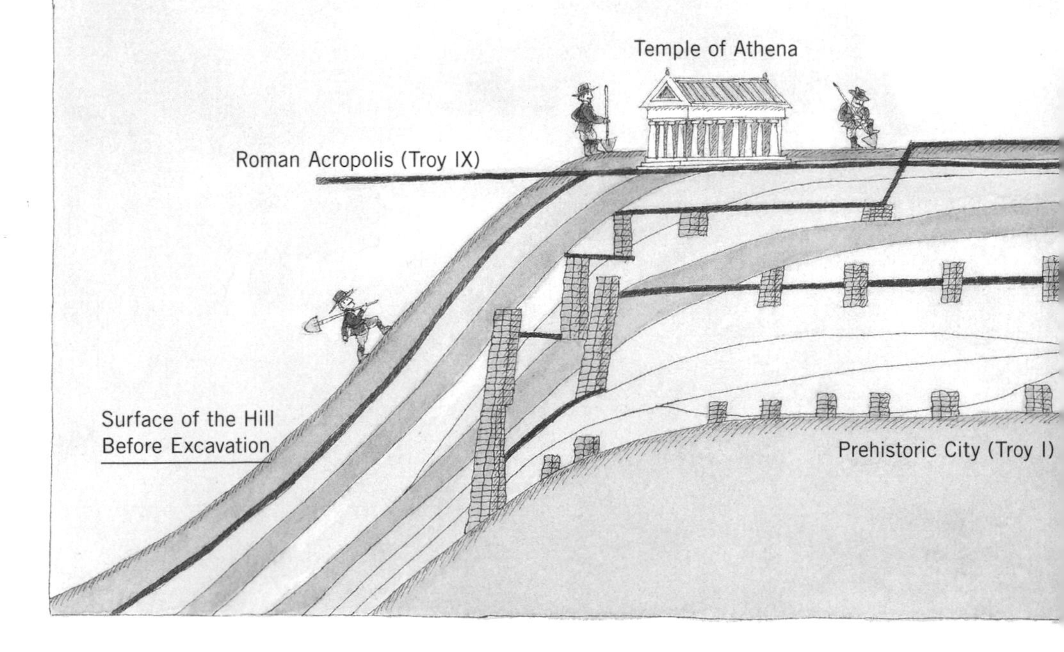

If you looked at the mound like an archaeologist, you'd see all the layers of your past life. You would keep a sharp eye out for anything that might help you to assign dates to the different strata. If, for example, you found your second-grade report card next to a plastic stegosaurus, you might guess that second grade was the year you were crazy about dinosaurs.

Now suppose your mother wanted to give away the red boots you loved when you were four. Suppose she tore apart your mound like a dog looking for a bone. What had once been an orderly mess would become chaos. The original layering, which made sense, would be lost forever.

What Heinrich Schliemann did at Hissarlik was quite a bit like that.

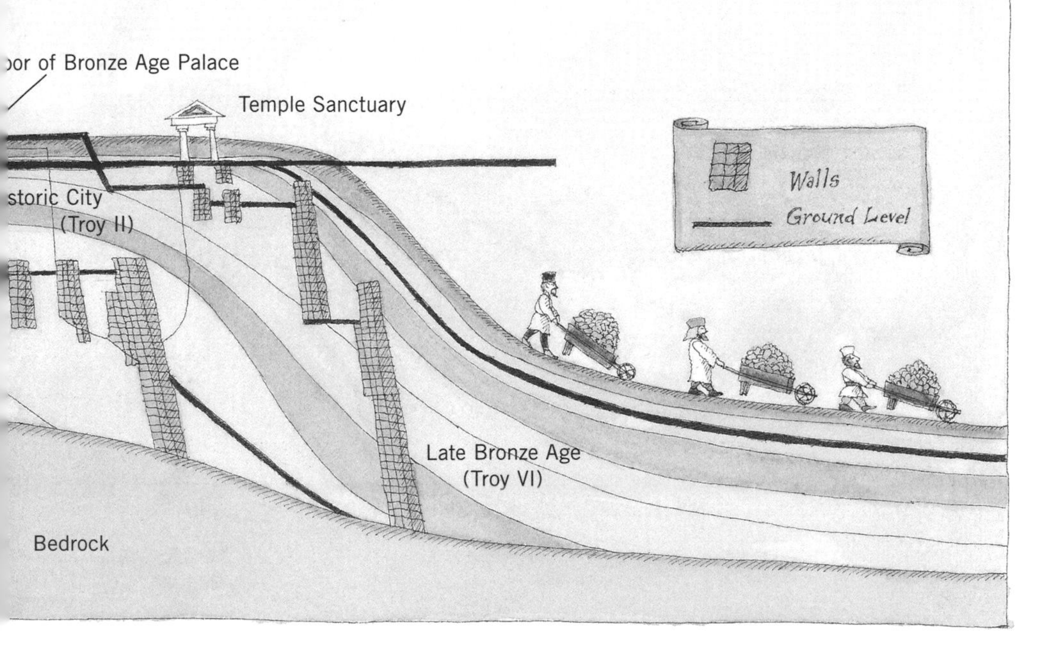

Calvert and Schliemann had agreed that whatever was found on Calvert's section of the mound would be divided between them, but the marble panel could not be cut in half. Heinrich wanted the whole thing. He offered to pay Frank Calvert for his share of the sculpture.

It was the end of their friendship. Since their first meeting, Frank Calvert had been unstinting with his knowledge and advice. Now Heinrich haggled like the cut-throat businessman he was. He succeeded in beating down the price, but he lost Calvert's respect. Later, when Calvert published criticisms of Schliemann's theories in historical journals, Schliemann felt betrayed.

Heinrich was publishing his discoveries almost as quickly as he made them. He expected the scholars of the world to applaud his labor; instead they accused him of jumping to conclusions. Heinrich raged at the criticism but continued to dig, assisted by his wife. At night the Schliemanns stayed up late, measuring, sketching, and recording their finds. Sophia, who had been so homesick in the grand hotels of Europe, accepted the primitive living conditions without a murmur, though she wore four pairs of gloves during the winter.

As Heinrich continued to study the mound, he came to believe that the second city from the bottom was the city of Homer's *Iliad.* It was a prehistoric city, with a paved ramp, a magnificent tower, and a huge gate, which Heinrich at once assumed was the "Scaean Gate" of *The Iliad.* The walls had been skillfully constructed, and—even more important—showed signs that the city had once been burned, like Homer's Troy.

Heinrich was outwardly delighted, and inwardly puzzled, by this city. He wanted nothing more than to believe that he had found Homer's Troy, but the city was very small—only about a hundred yards across. He found bronze and copper weapons, but the pottery found at this level was oddly primitive.

And there was no treasure. By now, Heinrich had been an archaeologist long enough to understand that he was supposed to be seeking knowledge, not treasure, and he was quick to assert that his only desire was to find Troy itself. But the lack of treasure was a nagging disappointment. Homer said that Troy was "rich in gold," but Heinrich had found little that was precious.

It was not until 1873 that Heinrich found the riches his heart craved. According to Heinrich, the treasure was found on the last morning of May. He was digging into a wall when he caught a glimpse of shining gold. Some instinct told him that there was a rich treasure hidden within the wall, and he resolved to dig it out for himself. He announced to the workers that it was his birthday (it wasn't) and told them to take the day off. He summoned Sophia to his side and told her to fetch her red shawl. Together, the husband-and-wife team worked to dig the artifacts out of the wall. There were thousands of precious objects: helmets and swords, vessels of gold and silver, shields, lances, vases, cauldrons, and jewelry. There were more than eight thousand gold rings; there were earrings and bracelets and necklaces and diadems.

Sophia bundled the treasure in her shawl and carried it back to their living quarters. Once they were alone together, Heinrich decked his beautiful wife in the golden diadem that had once kissed the brow of Helen of Troy.

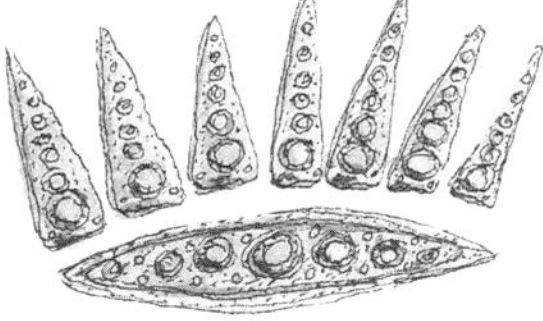

This is a good story. It is still found in books, but it is not true. For one thing, Sophia Schliemann was not with her husband on May 31. Her father had recently died, and she had gone to Athens for the funeral. As early as December 1873, Heinrich admitted to a friend at the British Museum that he had made up the story of Sophia and her red shawl. He explained that Sophia was becoming a gifted archaeologist and he wanted to encourage her by including her in the story of his great discovery.

Sophia's absence is not the only thing wrong with Heinrich's account of that day. Scholars who have examined Heinrich's notes also know that some of the objects in the treasure were found earlier—he had dated and photographed them *before* May 31. In fact, Heinrich combined several finds in order to make up what he called "Priam's treasure" after King Priam in *The Iliad*. His dramatic instinct demanded that the treasure be as lavish as possible, so he added to what he found.

Heinrich had a theory—or fantasy—about the treasure, and he wanted the world to share it. According to him, the treasure was hidden on the night Troy was invaded by the Greeks. Led by the crafty Odysseus, the Greek soldiers infiltrated the city, concealed within a wooden horse. Now they attacked with fire and sword. "The treasure was packed together at terrible risk of life, and in the greatest anxiety," wrote Heinrich. For Heinrich, a well-built city, signs of fire, and a hastily hidden treasure added up to one thing: Homeric Troy. He had solved what he modestly referred to as "the greatest and most important of all historical riddles."

Heinrich told the story of how he discovered Priam's treasure many times, and he never told it the same way twice. His shiftiness about the finding of the treasure was so noticeable that some of his fellow scholars suspected him of paying artists to make the precious objects and burying them himself, only to dig them up later. "Priam's treasure," which Heinrich thought would be the greatest triumph of his career, was also the greatest scandal.

• • •

A word about the treasure: It did not belong to King Priam, and it was not worn by Helen of Troy. Though the treasure is ancient and genuine, it predates the Trojan War by a thousand years. Modern archaeologists have since divided the site at Hissarlik into at least nine different Troys, dating from nine different periods of occupation. Heinrich's prehistoric city, second from the bottom, is generally known as Troy 2. Heinrich's dating, for both the treasure and the city, was a thousand years off: Troy 2 was not Homeric Troy.

It's easy to laugh now. To be "off" by a thousand years is to be pretty far "off." It's important to remember, though, that ancient artifacts do not come out of the ground with dates on them. Modern dating methods, such as radiocarbon dating, did not exist in Heinrich's time. In Heinrich's day, archaeologists had to figure out how old objects were by keeping track of how deep they were buried and by comparing them to other objects. Because the artifacts Heinrich was finding were so ancient, he didn't have objects with which to compare them. Later on, archaeologists came to date materials by creating a sequence of styles in pottery. Though Heinrich loved gold and precious stones, he was one of the first archaeologists to realize the importance of pottery. In this, he was ahead of his time.

In falsifying details of the treasure, however, he was doing his fellow archaeologists the kind of injury they find hard to forgive. All archaeologists, past and present, work together. Each object is a clue to the past, and archaeologists count on one another to pass on only the right clues. In hedging about exactly where and when the objects were found, Heinrich cheated his colleagues of the opportunity to learn the real history of his treasure.

·VI·

Though finding "Priam's treasure" was the thrill of a lifetime, it created a dilemma for Heinrich. According to the rules of the *firman,* half of the excavated goods belonged to the Turks. Heinrich had two choices: he could surrender half the treasure, or he could keep it a secret. He could not publish his great discovery without losing half of what he had found.

Either option was more than body and soul could bear. Heinrich could not wait to dazzle the public. He believed that the Trojan gold would bring him undying glory. The temptation to publish his finds was irresistible.

On the other hand, he could not stand to part with any of the treasure. Heinrich had a childish "finders-keepers" feeling about the Trojan gold. It was his connection to Homer, something he could hold in his hands. He had borne heat and dust and ridicule for it. He could not let it go.

The solution to this problem was a crooked one. Heinrich was neither the first nor the last archaeologist to resort to it. He smuggled the treasure out of the country. No one knows exactly how he did it: he may have been helped by the Calvert brothers or by members of Sophia's family, but the finding of the treasure was kept a secret. Once the gold left Turkey, Heinrich closed down the excavation and returned to Athens. There he photographed the treasure and wrote articles about its finding.

When the articles were published, Heinrich was in trouble, as he fully deserved to be. Though Greece and Turkey had been at odds for hundreds of years, the Greek government agreed that Schliemann ought to return the treasure to the Turks. When the authorities came to claim it, the treasure had vanished again. It seems likely that Heinrich divided it among the members of the Engastromenos family, who hid it in caves and barns.

Heinrich knew that he might go to jail, but didn't care. "I kept everything valuable that I found for myself and thus saved it for science," he wrote self-righteously. Guards surrounded the house. Policemen searched his belongings. The Schliemann bank accounts were frozen. Heinrich was questioned about the whereabouts of the treasure, but he kept his mouth shut. Only once did he come close to admitting his guilt. The Turks had arrested Effendi Amin, the watchman who had been hired to keep an eye on the Schliemann excavation. Heinrich felt no shame about stealing the treasure or smuggling it out of the country, but it distressed him that Effendi Amin should be put in jail for what he had done. He wrote to the Turkish government, pointing out that the loss of the treasure was not Amin's fault—he had done his best. He begged them, "in the name of humanity" to set Amin free.

There was a long court case. Eventually the Turks gave up and agreed that Heinrich should pay them for the treasure, a fine of fifty thousand francs. He joyfully sent five times that amount and a number of artifacts he did not greatly admire. Once again, his luck had held. Perhaps Hermes, the Greek god of thieves, protected him. Against all odds, he was able to keep the Trojan gold.

He was not, however, as celebrated as he had hoped to be. Many scholars felt that more evidence was needed before Hissarlik could be renamed Troy. Others found Heinrich's theories ridiculous, his stories preposterous. Cartoons and caricatures of the Schliemanns filled the newspapers.

All his life, Heinrich Schliemann was to irritate his colleagues. Though many scholars befriended him, he also made enemies—and his enemies simply could not stand him. They were disgusted by his romanticism, his boasting, his hysterical excitement over every new idea. It rankled that a grocer turned millionaire should unearth such staggering finds. Schliemann was a shrill and vulgar little man. What right had he to come up with theories?

Three years of frustration followed. Though he had gained fame, Heinrich had failed to dazzle the scholarly world, and he could not get permission to mount another excavation—this time at Mycenae. Because Mycenae was known to be a Bronze Age site, Heinrich hoped to find weapons and pottery similar to those he had found at Hissarlik. He also hoped to find the tomb of Agamemnon, the warrior king of *The Iliad*. Unfortunately, neither the Greek nor the Turkish government had any intention of letting him dig up anything. Who can blame them?

Heinrich argued and coaxed. It did no good. At last he resorted to bribery. He spent a huge sum of money to knock down an ugly tower that blocked a view of the Parthenon. The people of Athens had hated this eyesore for centuries, but no one had ever been willing to pay to get rid of it. Heinrich was willing to foot the bill. Shortly afterward, he received permission to dig at Mycenae. The rules of this *firman* were strict. Everything he found would belong to Greece—and he was limited to digging inside the city walls.

As it happened, Heinrich *wanted* to dig within the city walls. He believed that the royal tombs would be found inside Mycenae. He owed this belief to a Greek writer named Pausanias, who visited Mycenae in the second century of the Common Era.

Of course other scholars had read Pausanias, too, but they brought more knowledge to their reading. They knew that the city of Mycenae had once possessed *two* sets of walls, one inside the other. They reasoned that the space inside the inner wall was too small to hold the tomb of a great king. If royal tombs existed, they were certain they must lie somewhere between the inner and outer walls. It is probable the Greek government gave Schliemann permission to dig within the inner city walls because there was little chance of his finding anything there.

But Heinrich's hunch turned out to be an auspicious one—he found the tombs. Quite early on, he came upon a circle of stone markers. Inside the circle were tombstones that marked the entrance to narrow tunnels, leading straight down. At the bottom of the tunnels were underground chambers—shaft graves. Pausanias had mentioned five royal tombs, and Heinrich discovered exactly five shaft graves. (There were in fact six, but Heinrich trusted Pausanias completely; after he found the fifth grave, he stopped looking.)

As Heinrich had hoped, the graves were royal tombs, and they were magnificently rich. Fifteen royal corpses were heaped with gold. The men wore gold death masks and breastplates decorated with sunbursts and rosettes. The women were adorned with gold jewelry. All around the bodies were bronze swords and daggers inlaid with gold and silver, drinking cups made of precious stones, boxes of gold and silver and ivory. Once again, Heinrich was half-mad with enthusiasm. "I have found an unparalleled treasure," he wrote. "All the museums in the world put together do not possess one fifth of it. Unfortunately nothing but the glory is mine."

The tombs of Mycenae were even more spectacular than "Priam's treasure." The artifacts were exquisite, but that was not all—many of the artifacts matched *exactly* the descriptions found in Homer's *Iliad.* Wine cups, swords, jewels, bracelets, helmets—everything was in keeping with Homer's Bronze Age world. To crown it all, one of the gold-masked warriors had died in the prime of manhood. This, Heinrich felt certain, was the hero from *The Iliad,* the murdered Agamemnon. He knelt down and kissed the gold mask. Afterward, according to a famous story,

Heinrich telegraphed the king of Greece with the words, "I have gazed upon the face of Agamemnon."

This sounds like the sort of telegram Heinrich might have sent if he had thought of it, but the words are not his. Some other romantic soul invented the tale of the telegram—for once Heinrich himself was not responsible—and it has become part of the colorful Schliemann legend.

Was the dead king Agamemnon? No. Scholars have since determined that the shaft graves date from a hundred to three hundred years *before* the Trojan War. They were, however, Bronze Age graves. Heinrich was getting closer to the Homeric world he sought, but it still eluded him.

When a triumphant Heinrich published his findings about Mycenae, he revealed a lost world. The Bronze Age, that shadowy period between 1600 and 1100 BCE, had been drawn into the spotlight. The glory of that spotlight cast a golden glow over Heinrich Schliemann. He became a celebrity.

For the second time in his career, Heinrich's finds gave rise to scholarly debate. Many scholars felt that none of the shaft graves was ancient enough to be the resting place of the legendary king. One critic even thought that the "mask of Agamemnon" was meant to be an image of Jesus Christ. Heinrich grew testy when scholars refused to accept his bearded warrior as

Agamemnon. "All right," he snapped, "let's call him Schultze!" From that moment on, the warrior king was referred to as "Schultze." Schultze's mask continues to puzzle archaeologists up to the present day. It is unique in design, and some scholars consider it a forgery.

Nevertheless, Heinrich had made two of the greatest discoveries in archaeological history. He traveled widely during the next year, relishing his newfound fame. But even as he boasted, he was nagged by doubt. In studying the Mycenaean tombs, Heinrich formed a clearer idea of what Bronze Age artifacts looked like. Unfortunately, what they *didn't* look like were the artifacts he had found at Hissarlik. If Hissarlik and Mycenae were both remnants of Homer's heroic world, why were the sites so different from each other? Why weren't the treasures more alike?

In 1878, Sophia gave birth to a little boy, and Heinrich returned home for the christening. Heinrich had planned to call his son Odysseus, but changed his mind after his triumph at Mycenae. The infant was christened Agamemnon. Heinrich laid a book against the baby's head and read his newborn son a hundred lines of Homeric verse.

Shortly after his son's birth, Heinrich decided to return to Hissarlik. He wanted to re-examine the site. He was eager to find artifacts that would confirm his "Troy" as a Bronze Age city.

He applied to the Turkish government for a *firman* and, surprisingly, got it. He was even allowed to keep one third of whatever he found. During the 1879 excavations at Hissarlik, Heinrich was accompanied by a scholar and doctor named Rudolf Virchow.

Rudolf Virchow and Heinrich had a lot in common. Both loved Homer. The two men came from working-class backgrounds and were almost exactly the same age. Virchow's powers of energy and concentration were the equal of Heinrich's—and he shared Heinrich's fascination with human bones. In disposition, however, they were different: Heinrich was hotheaded, touchy, and dreamy; Virchow was thoughtful and self-contained.

Rudolf Virchow became a sort of father figure to Heinrich. He encouraged Heinrich to observe the land around Hissarlik, to take note of animal and plant life. He taught him to keep more accurate records and to think twice before jumping to conclusions. Virchow even advised Heinrich about personal matters. He reminded him to pay attention to Sophia and gave suggestions about what to feed the infant Agamemnon. Heinrich, who was not good at listening to other people, paid attention to Dr. Virchow—except when his new friend warned him against the dangers of bathing in icy water. Heinrich suffered from chronic earaches; Virchow told him, correctly, that his sea bathing would make the earaches worse. Heinrich ignored him.

Together Virchow and Schliemann tackled the mound at Hissarlik. More precious objects were found—Heinrich was almost getting used to finding treasure—but none of the objects resembled what he had found at Mycenae.

Heinrich decided to explore other Bronze Age sites. He was driven by two hungers—to learn more and to prove that his earlier theories were right.

He excavated at Orchomenus, another of the cities that Homer had described as "rich in gold." At Orchomenus, it was Sophia's turn to make a major discovery. She found a treasury room belonging to a legendary king, covered with intricate carvings of flowers and spirals. The chamber was so beautiful that the Schliemanns paid to have it restored.

At Orchomenus, Heinrich first hired Wilhelm Dörpfeld, whom later archaeologists were to call "Schliemann's greatest discovery." Dörpfeld was twenty-seven years old. He had been trained as an architect, and he had a genius for looking at ancient ruins and envisioning how they appeared long ago. Like Virchow, Dörpfeld was a good influence on Heinrich. He taught him how to excavate with care. Though he understood the science of archaeology far better than Heinrich did, Dörpfeld loved and admired the older man.

With Wilhelm Dörpfeld at his side, Heinrich set off for Tiryns, a city linked in myth with Hercules and the "warlike Diomedes" of *The Iliad.* Tiryns was Heinrich's third great triumph. With the help of Dörpfeld, he uncovered a majestic palace, decorated with wall paintings of Bronze Age men and women. The site yielded vast amounts of jewelry and pottery. In both size and decoration, it was the sort of palace that Heinrich had hoped to find at Hissarlik.

Heinrich was moving into his own palace around this time. He persuaded a famous architect to create a house that would celebrate Homer's heroic poetry. The "Palace of Troy" was a fantasy world, richly adorned with statues, murals, and Homeric inscriptions, "but it contained not one stick of comfortable furniture," complained his daughter Andromache.

The lack of comfort didn't bother Heinrich. Even in his sixties, he preferred to read and write standing up. Sophia and the children were forced to make the best of living in a museum. When Heinrich went away

on business, they packed a picnic basket and spread out their picnic on one of the hard mosaic floors.

Heinrich ruled over his Homeric palace like a king. He gave the servants names out of Homer and Greek mythology. He kept hens and pigeons and forbade anyone to kill them for food. No one was allowed to pluck the flowers in the garden—Heinrich had an odd theory that plants suffered when they were picked. Besides the birds, Heinrich doted on the family dog and a kitten he had rescued from Hissarlik.

During the last decade of his life, Heinrich received many visitors at his "Palace of Troy." He had grown more comfortable with people and entertained guests with kindness and generosity. He was an affectionate but demanding father, insisting that his children study hard, exercise vigorously, and speak foreign languages. His daughter Andromache wrote, "Throughout my own girlhood he would often get me up at five o'clock in the morning in winter to ride horseback five miles . . . to swim in the sea, as he himself did every day. . . .

Beneath these imperious traits Father was warmhearted and generous to a fault. He was humble, too, in his own way."

Humble? Perhaps not. When Heinrich wrote about his finds at Tiryns, he stated, "Once again the gods granted me . . . one of the most important archaeological discoveries ever made . . . from now till the end of time." Conceited though this sounds, there is truth in it. Though the palace of Tiryns is the least famous of Heinrich's three great triumphs, excavating it was a stupendous achievement. Once again, Heinrich crowed with triumph before the public, and the public responded with a mixture of catcalls and cheers.

Wilhelm Dörpfeld, who was responsible for the superb quality of the excavation work, stood in the wings, allowing Heinrich the limelight. Perhaps he understood that his time would come, that the older man would soon withdraw from the world of archaeology.

TROY VI
TROY III
TROY II

·VII·

During the last ten years of his life, Heinrich was often tired and sick. His earaches tortured him, and he suffered from malaria. In spite of his illness, he continued to travel, to swim, to write, and to dig.

In 1890, he returned once more to Hissarlik. It was his twelfth visit, and little had changed: it was still a place of owls and scorpions, poisonous snakes, wind and dust. On this particular visit, Heinrich did rather a mysterious thing: he began to excavate outside the walls of "his" Homeric Troy.

It may have been Dörpfeld's idea. Or it may have been Heinrich's—he had always been haunted by the fact that his prehistoric city was so small. In any event, once the two men dug outside the boundaries of what Heinrich had claimed was Troy, they came upon two buildings similar to the Bronze Age palace at

Tiryns. Inside, at last, they found what Heinrich had been looking for: pottery similar to that he had found at Mycenae. As if that were not enough, there was one last treasure—four stone axes of polished green jade and lapis lazuli. "I saw Pallas Athena in front of me," wrote Heinrich, "holding in her hands those treasures which are more valuable than all those I uncovered at Mycenae. . . . I cried for joy, fondled and kissed her feet. I thanked her from the bottom of my heart." He was later to smuggle the axes out of the country. He was not to be reformed.

Heinrich's last visit to Hissarlik uncovered more than treasure. At long last, he discovered the part of Hissarlik that matched the Bronze Age palace at Tiryns and the Bronze Age pottery he had unearthed at Mycenae. Historians are still wondering whether Schliemann fully understood what this latest find meant. What it meant, of course, is that the part of Hissarlik that he had maintained was Homeric Troy (Troy 2) did not date from the Bronze Age and was therefore *not* the Troy of Homer's *Iliad*. The books and articles that he had published were all wrong. Moreover, if this newly discovered layer of the mound (later called Troy 6) was Homer's Troy, he had thrown great heaps of it away. During his earlier attacks on Hissarlik, he had dug straight through the layer that he was trying to find. In his frenzy, he had destroyed buildings and artifacts that dated from the time of the Trojan War.

Wilhelm Dörpfeld, who excavated Troy 6 after Heinrich's death, had his own story about Heinrich's understanding of this latest find. He maintained that he broke the news to Heinrich and explained to the older man what the new findings signified: that Heinrich's earlier theories were wrong. "I discussed the matter with Schliemann, who listened carefully without saying much. He then retired into his own tent and remained incommunicado for four days. When he finally came out, he quietly said to me: 'I think you are right.'"

It was perhaps the most extraordinary moment of an extraordinary life.

In the autumn of 1890, Heinrich's earaches became agonizing. He lost nearly all of his sense of hearing. When doctors examined him, they found bony growths inside his ears. Rudolf Virchow advised Heinrich to have the growths cut out in a hospital in Germany. The operation was painful but successful. Afterward, Heinrich lay in bed reading the *Arabian Nights* (in Arabic, of course) and planning his next season's excavations.

The weeks that followed were lonely. Heinrich wrote a love letter to Sophia, praising her virtues. "At all times you were to me a loving wife, a good comrade . . . a dear companion on the road and a mother second to none." He was homesick. Against his doctor's orders, he made up his mind to leave the hospital and travel back to Athens, hoping to celebrate Christmas with his wife and children.

As he journeyed south, the pain in his ears returned and quickly grew worse. On Christmas Day 1890, he collapsed in Naples. Before a crew of doctors could agree how to treat his illness, he died.

The funeral was brilliant: Heinrich would have loved it. He was given a state burial, with a carriage drawn by eight black horses. Sophia recited Homer. Copies of *The Iliad* and *The Odyssey* were placed inside the coffin. Several hundred obituaries praised Schliemann's patience and industry, his unflagging energy, his uncanny hunches. William Gladstone, four-time prime minister of England, wrote that "Either his generosity without his energy, or his energy without his generosity might well have gained celebrity; in their union they were no less than wonderful." The inscription above the tomb read, *To the Hero Schliemann*.

Wilhelm Dörpfeld said, more simply, "Rest in peace. You have done enough."

What had he done? He had labored to prove that Homer's poetic world was true. He had done his energetic best to find Troy. Though most scholars now agree that Homeric Troy (Troy 6 or Troy 7) was located at Hissarlik, others await further proof. Today's archaeologists mourn the carelessness of Heinrich's excavations and the dishonesty that made him hedge about his finds. Heinrich Schliemann was a man who did things on a large scale, and his mistakes were not small ones.

Nevertheless, he took the world by storm. As ruthless as Achilles, as cunning as Odysseus, he rebelled against a commonplace fate. His hunger for a heroic life, his craving to *be* somebody, were not in vain. He did become rich; he did become famous; he did find lost cities and buried treasure. He spoke twenty-two languages. He wrote twelve books. Though he could not prove every detail of Homer's story, he changed the way archaeologists look at stories: he forced them to see that stories could unlock the door to great discoveries.

His excavations at Hissarlik, Mycenae, and Tiryns brought the Bronze Age to life. He once bragged: "Wherever I put my spade I always discovered new worlds for archaeology." It was true.

Many of his ideas were prophetic. Some of his most outlandish hunches—that the ancient people of Tiryns and Mycenae spoke Greek, for example—were later proved true by scholars who had the tools and training he lacked.

All his life, Heinrich was a lucky man, and he knew it. "I have had more luck than foresight in my life," he admitted. It could also be said that he made his own luck. He spared no effort and he never gave up. In the second half of his life, he had the good fortune to win the loyalty of three exceptional people: Sophia Schliemann loved and comforted him. Rudolf Virchow and Wilhelm Dörpfeld were his teachers, his counselors, and his friends.

Heinrich Schliemann wanted his life to be like a story—and it was. His rampant imagination changed archaeology forever. Some of the tales he told—like the tale of Sophia wrapping "Priam's treasure" in her red shawl—are everlasting, false though they may be. Heinrich's stories are chronic and irresistible. They are part of the Schliemann legacy. Storyteller, archaeologist, and crook—Heinrich Schliemann left his mark upon the world.

Notes and Comments

Though I have consulted all the books in the bibliography, the following sources were especially helpful:

Deuel, Leo. *Memoirs of Heinrich Schliemann: A Documentary Portrait Drawn from His Autobiographical Writings, Letters, and Excavation Reports.* Heinrich Schliemann from his own point of view. Schliemann's personality—his excitement, his conceit, his romanticism—manifests itself in every line. The editor, Leo Deuel, provides valuable background information.

Ludwig, Emil. *Schliemann: The Story of a Gold-Seeker.* Emil Ludwig was the first biographer to grapple with the great mound of writing that Schliemann left behind (two trunks full of materials written in ten different languages). When Ludwig was young, he met the aging Schliemann. After Schliemann's death, he interviewed Sophia Schliemann about her life with her husband.

Traill, David A. *Schliemann of Troy: Treasure and Deceit.* David Traill is the most skeptical of Schliemann's biographers. He has spent two decades studying Schliemann's life, working tirelessly to try to sort through Schliemann's half-truths and downright lies. Traill is a meticulous researcher and Heinrich Schliemann's sternest judge.

Moorehead, Caroline. *Lost and Found: The 9,000 Treasures of Troy: Heinrich Schliemann and the Gold That Got Away.* Caroline Moorehead's biography is also a story of the "Trojan Gold" and its disappearance during the Second World War. Though Moorehead is familiar with Traill's research, and rightly skeptical of Schliemann's stories, her view of the man himself is more tolerant than Traill's.

Wood, Michael. *In Search of the Trojan War.* Wood's book (and the accompanying videotapes) was enormously helpful in explaining the history and archaeology of Schliemann's Homeric Quest. Wood also has a knack for explaining archaeology to the layperson.

Poole, Lynn and Gray. *One Passion, Two Loves: The Story of Heinrich and Sophia Schliemann, Discoverers of Troy.* The Pooles interviewed Alex Mélas, the last living grandchild of Heinrich and Sophia Schliemann, who shared family stories with them and showed them documents that had never been published before. A good source for details about the Schliemanns' domestic life.

Chapter I
p. 3 "the mysterious and the marvelous" Deuel, p. 23.
p. 3 "Behind our garden . . ." Ibid., p. 24.
p. 4 "Father . . ." Ibid., p. 25.
p. 5 "my separation from my little bride" Ibid., p. 28.

Chapter II
p. 9 "The view of Hamburg . . ." Deuel, p. 39.
p. 9 "I would never again . . ." Ibid., p. 42.
p. 10 "flew like a seabird . . ." Ibid., p. 43.
p. 10 "I barely saved my life . . ." Ibid., p. 46.
p. 10 "gave my body over to the sharks" Ludwig, p. 24.
p. 11 "God must have chosen me . . ." Deuel, p. 51.
p. 11 "I felt reborn" Ibid., p. 52.
p. 11 "Friendships were made . . ." Ibid.
p. 12 "crowned with the fullest success" Ibid., p. 54
p. 13 "the greatest disaster" Ibid., p. 55.
p. 14 "swindling" "cunning" "immense love of money" Ibid., p. 71.
p. 14 Description of the falsified diary noted by Traill, p. 12.
p. 15 "I lay more dead than alive. . . ." Deuel, pp. 83–84.

Chapter III
p. 18 "All through the war . . ." Moorehead, p. 46.
p. 18 "How is it possible . . ." Ludwig, p. 74.
p. 18 "I cannot remain . . ." Ibid., p. 79.
p. 18 "How is it . . ." Payne, p. 77.
p. 21 "downright falsehoods . . ." Deuel, p. 127.

Chapter IV
p. 29 "the fatherland of my darling Homer" Moorehead, p. 70.
pp. 30–31 "It is very possible . . ." Traill, pp. 45–46.
p. 34 "I completely shared . . ." Deuel, p. 153.

p. 34 "The beautiful hill of Hissarlik . . ." Ibid., p. 154.
p. 35 "Frank Calvert, the famous archaeologist . . ." Traill, p. 56.
p. 35 "a braggart and bluffer" Deuel, p. vii.

Chapter V

p. 37 "because otherwise she cannot love . . ." Traill, p. 67.
p. 37 "a good and loving heart" Moorehead, p. 92.
p. 38 "Why do you wish . . ." "Because my parents . . ." Ludwig, pp. 114–115.
p. 39 "friend for life" "dearest husband" "adored wife . . ." Poole, p. 129.
p. 39 "I knew I loved . . ." Moorehead, p. 99.
p. 41 "Troy . . . was sacked twice . . ." Kennedy, pp. 94–95.
p. 43 "It was an entirely new world . . ." Deuel, p. 220.
p. 49 "The treasure was packed . . ." Ibid., p. 207.
p. 49 "the greatest and most important . . ." Ibid., p. 197.

Chapter VI

p. 54 "I kept everything valuable . . ." Deuel, p. 213.
p. 55 "in the name of humanity" Moorehead, p. 141.
p. 58 "I have found . . ." Ibid., pp. 167–168.
p. 59 "I have gazed . . ." Wood, p. 68.
p. 60 "All right, let's call him Schultze!" Moorehead, p. 170.
p. 62 "Schliemann's greatest discovery" Deuel, p. 287.
p. 63 "Palace of Troy" [Schliemann named his palace Ilíou Mélathron, which can be translated as either "Palace" or "Hut" of Ilium (or Troy).] Ibid., p. 281.
p. 63 "but it contained . . ." Ibid., p. 347.
pp. 64–65 "Throughout my own girlhood . . ." Ibid.
p. 65 "Once again the gods granted me . . ." Ibid., pp. 314–315.

Chapter VII

p. 68 "I saw Pallas Athena . . ." Deuel, p. 344.
p. 69 "I discussed the matter . . ." Moorehead, p. 235.
pp. 69–70 "At all times . . ." Ibid., p. 229.
p. 70 "Either his generosity . . ." Deuel, p. 352.
p. 70 "Rest in peace . . ." Traill, p. 297.
p. 71 "Wherever I put my spade . . ." Moorehead, pp. 212–213.
p. 72 "I have had more luck . . ." Deuel, p. 8.

Bibliography

Bahn, Paul G., editor. *Cambridge Illustrated History of Archaeology.* Cambridge: Cambridge University Press, 1996.

Braymer, Marjorie. *The Walls of Windy Troy: A Biography of Heinrich Schliemann.* New York: Harcourt, Brace, 1960.

Caselli, Giovanni. *In Search of Troy: One Man's Quest for Homer's Fabled City.* New York: Peter Bedrick, 1999.

Ceram, C. W. *Gods, Graves, & Scholars: The Story of Archaeology.* 2nd rev. ed. New York: Vintage, 1986.

Deuel, Leo. *Memoirs of Heinrich Schliemann: A Documentary Portrait Drawn from His Autobiographical Writings, Letters, and Excavation Reports.* London: Hutchinson, 1978.

Duchêne, Hervé. *Golden Treasures of Troy: The Dream of Heinrich Schliemann.* Discoveries series. New York: Abrams, 1996.

Homer. *The Iliad.* Translated by Richmond Lattimore. Chicago: University of Chicago Press, 1961.

Homer. *The Odyssey.* Translated by Robert Fagles. New York: Viking, 1996.

Kennedy, Maev. *The History of Archaeology.* Surrey, England: Quadrillion/Octopus, 1998.

Ludwig, Emil. *Schliemann: The Story of a Gold-Seeker.* Boston: Little, Brown, 1931.

Mohen, Jean-Pierre, and Christiane Eluère. *The Bronze Age in Europe.* Discoveries series. New York: Abrams, 2000.

Moorehead, Caroline. *Lost and Found: The 9,000 Treasures of Troy: Heinrich Schliemann and the Gold That Got Away.* New York: Viking, 1994.

Payne, Robert. *The Gold of Troy: The Story of Heinrich Schliemann and the Buried Cities of Ancient Greece.* New York: Funk & Wagnalls, 1959.

Poole, Lynn and Gray. *One Passion, Two Loves: The Story of Heinrich and Sophia Schliemann, Discoverers of Troy.* New York: Crowell, 1966.

Traill, David A. *Schliemann of Troy: Treasure and Deceit.* New York: St. Martin's, 1995.

Tyler, Deborah. *The Greeks and Troy.* New York: Dillon, 1993.

Ventura, Piero, and Gian Paolo Ceserani. *In Search of Troy.* Morristown, N.J.: Silver Burdett, 1985.

Wood, Michael. *In Search of the Trojan War.* New York: Facts on File, 1985.